THAT RAIN WE NEEDED

That Rain We Needed

Poems

Sam Barbee

Press 53
Winston-Salem

Press 53, LLC
PO Box 30314
Winston-Salem, NC 27130

First Edition

Cover design by Kevin Morgan Watson

Cover art, "Window in Bodie," Copyright © 2003
by Maribeth Galie, used by permission of the artist.

Photographs for sections I and II, Copyright © 2016
by Chris Almerini, used by permission of the artist.

Author photo by Joanna Ritchie Britt

Printed on acid-free paper
ISBN 978-1-941209-40-0

To Jan,
my partner and confidant in all things

Special thanks to Edgar A, Walt, Thomas S,
Ezra, the Johns, the Williams,
and, without a doubt, Keith Flynn

Acknowledgments

The poet wishes to thank the following magazines, journals, and anthologies where these poems, or versions of them, appeared.

Asheville Poetry Review: "The Crab Killer"

Award Winning Poems (The North Carolina Poetry Society): "Adult Kiss," "Tomato"

Charlotte Poetry Review: "Valentine's Day"

Crucible: "Coffee Talk"

Georgia Journal: "Summer Solstice"

The Indian River Review: "The Best Equipment"

Kostroma: "Drip Line"

Lonzie's Fried Chicken: "The Route Man"

Main Street Rag: "Red Planet" and "Lost Frequency"

Maryland Poetry Review: "Current"

Mount Olive Review: "Our Father's Son"

No Straight Roads: "Thyme"

The North Carolina Poetry Society 50th Anthology: "Raisins"

The Poet's Page: "Five O'clock Shadow"

Pembroke Magazine: "visitation"

The Southern Poetry Anthology, Volume VII: North Carolina: "What's Not Left"

Wellspring: "Poems She Read," "Wallace Park"

What the Fiction: "Seven Colors"

Windhover— Journal of Christian Literature: "And She Cries Every Sunday"

Zuzu's Petals: "Raisins"

Contents

III– That Rain We Needed

I

What's Not Left

Tint

My mother dyed her hair—
I was adopted that next day—
processed, approved by all,
made-to-order with Dad's red hair.

Saturday nights, I watched her
bend above a basin soaking
red tints into gray, rinsing away
the lack of 50s perfection.

Dad displayed me to friends and family,
a boy to teach all he knew.
She rocked me through twilight
with lullabies, making me her own.

Their first child had died,
born blue and silent.
Number two was sponged away.
Determined to improvise,

My mother dyed her hair—
immersing each strand in auburn tints,
hoping to look the part. As I grew,
teenage pastimes replaced her.

My father discovered electric trains, or
took me fishing. Through attrition,
we abandoned her. The gambit fell apart,
leaving another shadow to cradle.

Her hair found truer color. Toward the end,
strokes and strike outs paled her prayers.
I wrapped myself in the quilt she never started,
as my orphan's life began again.

Our Father's Son

Your stone waits, aligned
with other small ones.
Scrubbed clean. Polished each Easter.
Yet, no third-day revival
for you: I portrayed
that reincarnation.
                                        I
re-hear your impossible odds:
born inverted, untimely from
your mother's womb. Unkind trade
of a cradle for a tomb . . . you,
our father's son.

I missed out on wisdom you
might have shared: on girls, on shaving,
your cheering while I learned to drive.
Lived out that sibling fantasy,
but had things gone better for you,
we would never have met.
                                        Me
the adopted boy: play piano, catch the ball.
Fill your place at the table.
Be smart. Grow tall.
I crumble easily . . . me,
our father's son.

Do not misunderstand—he has loved me well,
and to his ends—nothing wrong here.
As we gather before you, his hands hang loose.
I turn from him at your grave.
That wince, that grimace I can never
soothe. I feel silly here.
                                        You
conceived as the pride and joy.
I must improvise in your void.
He strokes my shoulder: heir
apparent to it all . . .
the red-haired, blue-eyed boy.

4

Moving Day

I cannot remember the shape
of the moon that particular night
but do recall swelter and how
humidity snapped between my fingers.

Pop Pike's balding head bobbed
above the Kelvinator, carrying
a distinct astronomy in his face,
bifocals clamped firm like a pair of stars.

Granddad Barbee, never to be outdone,
hoisted boxes. He and my dad bickered,
jousting with hand trucks as
grandmothers chirped in the porch swing.

That June's family ensemble—
a reliable galaxy of nurses,
and backwoods prophets,
mechanics and clumsy magicians—

all assembled assisting our move,
to a smaller house, porch, kitchen.
Mature water oaks and a tin garage
proved two of its few graces,

but all make up my black and white
constellation of faces in the first place
I knew as home, where I fleshed out grace,
and first debates with solitude were prepared.

The Crab Killer

After church and fried chicken,
we went fishing most every Sunday.
Seldom missed incoming tide.
In his folding chair, webbing frayed and green,
Daddy smoked those Camels.
I chased my beach ball, primary colors
spinning down the hard sand.
I scrawled words and pictures
into the gray canvas.

Daddy summoned me, hiding his latest catch.
As I scrambled to him, he tossed a crab toward me. . . .
and, during my gallop from this thing,
I knew it must be gaining.
Looking back, I could count
my steps in the sand.
He motioned to trust him once again.
I trembled as he pointed to the creature
impaled on his fishing knife,
wincing as he pinned
the turquoise shell
to the beach.

Its eyes held no secrets.
Each leg scrambled,
disabled by the blade:
crawling, digging—attempting escape,
pinchers opening and reclamping,
again and again.
I squinted up.
Daddy's hat blocked the sun.

What is that?

Ah, only an old she-crab.

Is it dead?

Oh, just about.

What do she-crabs eat?

Little boys who wander. . . .

The tall fisherman gouged the shiny hook
through a cold shrimp's eye.
He owned the water's edge.
As he cast, breakers exploded around him.
I deflated my beach ball
and sat by his lawn chair.
The horizon, cluttered with cypress,
swept up the sun.

Adult Kiss

I was young and
mother always
made her face
with lipstick sassy-red.
Before leaving,
she would kiss

a fresh tissue.
I became jealous
of that perfect imprint,
tossed in
the waste basket—
affection meant for me.

Now when my wife
departs my arms
each morning—made up—
I am portioned
a glossy peck and
I transfer it to

a tissue: a rosy shadow
smeared for saving
and cashing in that night.
At times, life
finds its own way
of settling accounts.

High Fidelity

Stilled in my single bed,
stuffed lion protecting me,
the television became silent.
My father rattled about the bathroom.
The medicine cabinet closed, then the clank
of the brush swabbing in his soap cup,
the swash in the basin, then conclusive pop
of the stopper, water and murky remnants

of another day down the drain.
Sequestered in the kitchen, mother read
one of her thick books, on a stool
at the wooden island . . . sipping tea
and smoking Lucky Strikes after the hour
when she thought I dreamed. Those nights,
he sought her, beneath that single bulb
dangling on two twisted wires, bright face

glowing with an incandescent blush:
still his debutante, still her prince.
He would clasp her hand and caress it
against his smooth cheek and chin.
She giggled a promise to only finish
the next chapter and rinse her face.
In their bedroom, he dialed the radio until
its rasp played his favorite, scratchy jazz.

Mark of the Z

Zorro—my boyhood hero:
incognito with a gleaming sword
to serrate the wicked and corrupt,
a black stallion rearing on the ridge,
cape fluttering in full moonlight.

That Easter, with sash and hilt,
with a stiff crepe myrtle rapier,
I hacked grandmother's tulips,
lavender, white and pink
slain over the garden bank.

Like a masked savior, I faced
their pastel danger and sliced it
to its knees. During my romp,
a hand clamped my shoulder,
dismantled my triumphant pose.

My aunt led me from the battlefield
to the shadow of a gable. After
her finger's lunge disarmed me,
we collected each vanquished bandit,
then balanced them in a crystal vessel.

My grandmother sat at the dining table
as I entered with the arrangement.
Her head tilting, she gazed to my aunts
who turned their backs, busying themselves
with Sunday lunch. Her slender fingers

slid the blossoms onto the center leaf.
Do you like 'em? She whispered, *Yes.*
I grinned, and nodded during her hug,
Yes, I do, eyes bright like the cut-glass
crucible poised in the noon sun.

Twin Beds

I revered their chamber,
its frost in summer—
bright strength in winter.

My Grandparents slept there:
his gold pocket watch on the bureau,
her red bonnet on the chair.

But after Jemmima died, all seasons,
all holidays, came and went.
He gave up on the room's comforts.

One summer visit, it was decided
I would sleep in his honey's bed—
the first to unmake the crisp linens

and pretty gingham spread. In sparse wattage
of a bedside lamp, he rubbed himself
with curious liquids from brown bottles.

His spearmint and vanilla pierced my prayers.
Twilight sprinkled the bedroom sheers.
Nightbreeze wavered webs of curtain lace.

I witnessed his confessions, and, somewhere
in that midnight pitch, I lost myself
between shadows on the plaster ceiling.

At dawn, Granddad ventured to the garden.
I remade her bed, and straightened his bottles,
making sure each cork was snug.

After Murder

On the corner store's magazine rack
a *Police Gazette* scowled at patrons—
black and white, grim, grotesque.
It documented three slain children
in a bathtub, contorted, curled
in spewed blood. There among
Look, Life, Mad glared this chronicle
of how a father became butcher.
Unable to read big words,
my toes curled inside my sneakers—

heart in stasis—I could not pivot.
The store's jonquil bouquets mixed
with the frost off the freezer doors.
Had they talked back? Been late for dinner?
Not made their bed? I stared at betrayal
seeping from torsos, refocusing
on the word *Father*. My imagining
interrupted by the clang of a cash drawer,
Dad's palm dangled at my shoulder.
Let's go, Buck.

Undressing for my time in the tub,
mother felt my pale brow—
I nodded all was well as she slid me
into the warm envelope of water.

Get clean, now.
On the wall hung a sampler, yellow stitch work,
Cleanliness Is Next To Godliness.
                            I clutched soap
and rag, scrubbing each knee in deliberate circles.
I heard the television buzz on
and Dad rock back into his recliner.
His cigarette lighter flicked open, and,
with a snap of his wrist, the familiar blue flame
was born, then snuffed.

Trick Photography

When my mother became ill,
I never heard the surgeon
lay it out for him, but cures
were left out of the conversation.
My dad found a comfortable chair,
knowing no one would debate fairness,
no final-frame savior would
cruise in to rescue his damsel.

Saturday night, we gathered before
the black and white television
to watch a movie, with an inevitable scene
when the hero would take flight,
a mountain collapse, or Moses part the sea.
Clad in my robe and slippers,
cuddled beside my mother,
I asked, *Is that real?*

She smiled at him, secure in his recliner.
In turn my dad would respond,
Trick photography, —his explanation
to many things we watched,
needing context, in terms he knew.
Grinding his pipe, he nodded,
They can do anything
with that movie magic.

Current

His forum encircled our kitchen table.
There my father laid down his law on politics,
religion, and life's other dilemmas.
When feeling out-debated by us,
he relied on his tradesman's metaphors
and similes grounded in absolute truth:
it's like electricity—can't smell it, hear it, see it.

The school path home bordered a glen
splotched with sycamores. Years before,
cows grazed there. Now goats frolicked,
penned by a sagging electric fence,
rusted *Danger* signs stapled to cedar posts.
My pals and I challenged the wire, wielding
shorter and shorter sticks to touch the twisted strands.

And that bold day came they convinced me
to extend an index finger and test the shock,
to butt bravery against *can't smell it, hear it, see it.*
That one reckless moment, I lunged and sensed
smoke bellow from my ears, marrow frying.
I torqued to retract flesh and tumbled
over a fallen branch, jolting each clumsy nerve.

Facedown in the weeds, I examined my uncharred finger—
there was no voltage, only schoolmates' laughter.
As blood trickled down my chin I heaved the branch at the goats. . . .
Through a fitful supper hour, my tongue massaged
my sore lip, and I gazed at my father eager
for some new wisdom, faith in unseen things
reestablished by his untouchable laws.

Mowing

I stood straight in high grass, noon sun
bestowing my chance to come of age.
Gray hair hidden with bottle tint,
my aunt sipped ice tea, holding a tissue
to the glass. I stood erect before her
in the shade as she reclined in a chaise lounge
reviewing safety switches and mower gears.
She warned of wasps and hornets.
Briars. Roughly defined tulip beds

that once provided color for cut crystal
were to remain untouched. I recalled
crimson summers when junipers
crowded this garden's rock walls.
And my Crayola marks on their television screen.
A baseball through the front window. . . .
The mower sputtered into musical whir.
I began symmetrical journeys over dandelions
and tame bermuda. My aunt, draped in black,

nodded. Never from her view,
I honored each overgrown flower bed.
After blue granite borders were carved out,
she stood over their frayed integrity,
her hands clasped. Returning
to a silver maple's shadow, she poured us
both some cool tea and encouraged me
to sit and chat in the grass beside her. From there,
we admired the sweet clipped design of spring.

Summer Solstice

That June they boarded
my cousin Cheryl
with us at the coast.

Cheryl spent her days
sewing baggy dresses and
reading thick books,

but at dusk she draped herself
in sleeveless frocks,
and doused her pale shoulders

with vanilla extract. Those evenings
I sat on a stone bench in the back yard
and pondered her. The night sky

glistened with bright pinpoints
through water oak boughs as
she rocked on the back porch

behind the rusted screen
where potted gardenias flourished.
Cheryl was allowed to sip red wine

in the darkness. As her days
tightened, and her season short,
she often cried there.

I still hear her transistor radio and
cringe from the smoldering citronella.
As the streetlights brightened,

she sneaked out her tobacco.
With each breath, her face glowed.
My parents whispered

behind the kitchen curtain's lace.
I marveled, seduced by her boldness, and
watched the smoke swirl round her face.

Poems She Read

God had driven me to this critical task.
I was prepared to right this primal injustice.
He had afflicted me with this growth,
filling in freckled vistas from my
forearm to my calf. Bathing me,

my mother tried to scrub away her recognition,
but broken-hearted kissed my forehead.
In my bedroom's silence, I could lie motionless
and sense the stubble sprouting. I knew
my resolve was capable of anything

to keep her touch, anything to postpone
that talk with my Dad: man-to-man,
face-to-slick-face. Poised before my mirror
framed with baseball cards, I counted
the clustered follicles. Stainless edges

of the scissors cool against my thigh.
As I snipped back tiny shoots of manhood,
I watched the blonde fibers float
onto hardwood, and felt unworthy:
sure banishment from mother's labyrinth.

No more bath time chats or reading me poems.
No more toweling my unmuscled chest.
I maintained this secret effort for weeks, but
my diligence dulled. And, after his workdays,
Dad had a newfound energy. Each spring evening,

he wanted to play catch. He showed me
the slow curve, the knuckler, and helped
ease me into my summer. Mother receded
into the kitchen, shucking corn or frying veal.
There were times I saw her gossamer outline

watch us from behind the French door sheers.
We held hands to grace dinner, but when conversation
lapsed, she told me of old poems she had re-read
and new ones she would like to share. That summer
my Dad also began to let me watch him shave.

AM Radio

It was that time I longed for:
hours after nine, prayers recited,
I clicked on my transistor AM radio.
WOWO, 1010, Fort Wayne, Indiana,
provided a soundtrack for dreaming.

My grandfather's '49 Plymouth
sailed us to our secret places,
behind barns, beneath oaks
dripping Spanish moss as the silver
bumpers rolled through high grass fields.

The wide back seat became
the late-night bleacher
for any adolescent debates:
ecology, or Vietnam, or angel's hair.
Flawless June sky spilling stars across our skin,

"Magical Mystery Tour," "I Am The Walrus,"
dismissed day-lit-dreams of French verb conjugations,
geometry formulas, making the next team.
After sundown, WOWO's signal
always came in clear, and ivory dials

and tubes of that old radio
served us with enough light
to make the dash shimmer
like our private ocean—"Strawberry Fields Forever"
played as I imagined my Indiana girl

listening: so beautiful and smart,
baseball-lover, Beatle fan. Our airway pure,
I whispered to her, and never lost resolve,
between the downbeats of "All You Need Is Love"
before WOWO was white noise,

and the Indiana girl, powder in my eyes.
Submerged in our own intricate passions
stronger than any catechism, we sailed
into our own loving pledges, and somewhere,
submerged inside our intimate adventure, we meant them.

Iron Cross

My round skim-board, crafted
in wood shop, gleamed full of two
colors that made my mother shudder.
Blues and greens don't go together.
They'll look all wrong to people who know.

I had hatched another breach for debate:
cleaved by our rigid hues, we blood-let
during disputes . . . made up over meals.
My spherical project was perfect for
shoreline ripples leveling over hard sand.

Its wicked green paint curved out into quarters
with a painted cobalt blue surfer's cross over it
I hopped on top, and spun in flattened breakers,
color spokes rotating across toothless surf,
gliding through summer, performing limited

repertoire of tricks and turns. Families
with fat babies perched along dunes. My mother
watched over sunglasses, wry smile leaking.
The board's pattern looked like a dogwood petal,
me crowning the center, balancing my hard-won mettle.

Wallace Park

Those hot days around the diamond,
we would bring out a new white baseball,
discard the wrinkled wrappings.
We pitched and hit, all afternoon
circling burlap bases, showing our skills
to flat-chested girls. We hammered
the smooth leather off many tight-stitched things,
charmed their roundness in summer dust.

Under mush and silt, behind the rusting mesh
where the less-talented watched us,
remains a shrine where only players
claimed privilege—the bat graveyard.
There we buried short lengths
of our Louisville Sluggers,
snapped above an adolescent grip,
just below the polished sweet spot.
New bats, old bats, all bats—
turned-over too quick, or fooled by
a slow curve at dusk.
                    No need to count steps,
I know the direct route, like those
familiar trails inside other cemeteries.
I rustle the paper and Pepsi tops,
scrape back oak leaves, and locate
rows of round oak handles.
Bat dimensions burned in each knob—
30, 32, 34, 36—notches in our teenage
progressions.
                    Our girls offered kisses
after every homerun, between long innings.
For the ceremony, we encouraged them to hold
the broken stobs as we impaled
the splinters into the sparkle of clover.

I now study this geography from the crest
of a turfless bank, cluttered by cinders and debris.
The perfect stream, the eastern boundary,
is choked off, full of weeds and diesel.
The backstop remains, panels
of galvanized vines, shaded by water oaks.
Spanish ivy crowds the benches
where we rested our oversized gloves
and summertime hearts. The plywood
home plate has rotted, but a cypress
I once pruned with one left-handed swat
of a bright Rawlings ball stands proud
and plumb, dead-away center field.

This humid afternoon,
I still inhale that season, when
command of the day's perfect pitch,
and first love under starlight,
proved enough of truth
to share between the freshness
of a newly mowed center field
and the cypress by the stream.

Armed Forces

NBC blared, "Kennedy is dead."
I was out of school: Thanksgiving Holidays—
turkey legs and stuffing—
not much traffic—not the usual neighbors walking.
My dad sat on the back steps, and
worked up enough saliva to expel a bloody paste
onto the ground. *Curse this hurt.*
The dentist had yanked his final incisors.

All his teeth had withered from suffering fevers
from malaria and diphtheria in North Africa.
You know, the President was a veteran,
just like me. Both battlin' that Axis.
He had hard evidence: black and white snapshots
of pyramids—the Sphinx—bare-breasted native girls—
elephants—Staff Sergeant of the motor pool
that drove Rommel from the dunes—the Victory Story.

I hope they hang that son-of-a-bitch. Then,
he motioned for me to come close. *Son, little fellas*
shouldn't say grown-up words like that. Okay?
I nodded and hugged him. His body stiffened.
You're a good boy. . . . I just hope
that'll be enough. Curse this hurt. . . .
His stale cigarette breath made me gasp. He spit again,
bloody paste curdling in dust. *Curse this hurt.*

That night snug in bed, the television still buzzed.
My lips silently formed the new phrase:

                              son-of-a-bitch

into the wrinkles of my white pillow.

Rhapsody in Blue

Before a diagnosis could name his angst,
before any counselor explained it away,

my father's jazz dreams were
wallowed out by a dull needle,
hollowed out with daunting phrases.
He could name off Basie's count,
knew the luster of Miller's pearls,
enjoyed frenzied structure of Charlie Parker.

At my age, a clarinet was a horn.
A timpani, a big drum, but
the Gershwin album cover
syncopated each scarlet note
with a dark Parisian girl,
cleavage draped in a sheet.

As he dropped the stylus onto
the black vinyl, his eyes lifted
from his soul-crushing job,
from the warp of our imperfect home.
The ebony clarinet's playful murmur
calmed his visions of his daily war,

the big band soothing his scars.
and provided me reverie of the girl.

The Route Man

He serviced the best territory
in Wilmington, the Port City.
Daily he dialed and delivered
tea and coffee, tobaccos, sundries
and stuffed toys. On Saturdays,

he converted his small tin garage
into a dirt-floor stockroom.
Always home by sundown,
Mr. B. dined with his wife and his boy.
And then came his time with his trains.

In the back room of the house,
on grass-green plywood, silver tracks wound
through plastic neighborhoods and feathery trees.
Train cars chugged around the room:
over bridges he had engineered,

into tunnels he had mined,
through flashing railroad crossings
he had constructed—the route man controlled
these scaled-down acres—life
operated on his schedule.

Mile after miniature mile,
the Lionel diesel puffed and churned.
When his sick wife became sicker,
Mr B. sold his trains to pay sitters
and bills from specialists.

Platforms and mountain ranges were
dismantled. Rats nested in the rusting
tin garage and absorbed all
out-of-date stock. The best route man
in Wilmington was waived by

a Company Man from Raleigh
for *Excessive Absenteeism*.
After that the Jewel Tea Co.
noticed a slight increase in
good-customer complaints.

What's Not Left

Hands clasp the Tube Rose can
after she has heard me. The snuff's
pungent scent spills off her breath.
She picks at doilies protecting her
upholstered chair's threadbare arms
and answers my questions, a tissue
dabbing corners of her lips.

All things must leave you one day—
even her lemon-yellow canary,
like his emerald mate a season ago—
Weeping may stay the night, but
joy comes in the morning.
Past the empty hanging cage,
she motions out the window, and

explains the pair are together, there
in some bird heaven, tending one another,
exalting in a persimmon tree, in a grove,
near a calm lake where old fishermen
offer them skewered gills of their catch,
and toss the long-day's leftover
worms onto the shore.

Raisins

for E.L.P

Having ground up
their final juices of tenderness,
I forgot that all flavor fades:
that decent delight is portioned
by good fortune, or those special folks.

After my grandfather, who re-wrote
the Bible, surrendered his last fistful
of raisins to the black and white goats, I
learned to endure without easy sweetness.
During our last summer,

we re-tarred the coup, burned out wasps.
Between pitchers of sun-brewed tea,
he explained dragonflies and why roses
need each thorn. Late afternoons, a
hewn oak handle churned rock salt into chocolate.

Sickness drained him away. I accept
the fact he drank heavy, and that it killed him.
I lost his New Testament notes, but salvaged
the bifocals from his desk and have protected
them all these years. I refuse to misplace

the imprint of the calloused palm that helped
me straddle the cedar rail of the pasture fence
when we counted wrens fluttering through threads
of sunset under low sourwood branches while the goats
butted and danced in his vineyard's last light.

II

The Shade That Saves Me

Palm Sunday

Rain continues to pound the day. You marvel
at robins hiding beneath lily blooms.
I rely on little more from you, my child, yet

in secret hope for more. Worms seep onto
the asphalt drive to save from drowning
in sod—those birds spare will fry into crisps

when sun dries the vineyards, and wind carries
away the dogwood's final rusted blossom.
Forsythia leaves shimmer in morning's gloom.

We gather, the greenest branch of this family,
around a varnished table and clash over lunch—
who sits where, your cup colors, big-boy silverware—

any non-critical accouterment. I bite at you with
my non-clinical phrases, strike back with my awkward
roaring. And then,

                         there you are, darling son,
huddled and scorned, panicked in midday dust,
struggling with desire to trust me again.

From the window, I weigh the yellow sky.
Can we wash our hands of one another
so easily, even with the silver rain?

I have crushed your budding glory, stunted
your limbs with blunt rage. Will life allow me
to cushion your journey with fresh-cut palms,

with daises pied or violets blue, bathe you in rare
fragrance, exult your victories as saints sleep,
their tombs intact in distant mountains?

visitation

          as in most
matters of homage, one benign
noble always endures. it is late
spring at my house—the castle
you helped form. post-Easter:
dogwood blossoms cure in the grass.

          this season, years ago,
I admired your frailty, the way
you caved in at her graveside.
it was ok to escape the crowd, split
the groomed boxwood, and stride out
of there, my shining father, on
your own, shunning comfort.

          that bitter mourning
should make tonight easier
on me . . . having seen how it's done—
that and our distances. but for your
worship, I must rely on strength from
numbers: friendly faces at arm's length,
unsure hands that know how I feel.
new family. old friends.

          before we visit, I kiss
my child's brow as he whispers *Amen* over
colorful vegetables. he chews them well,
yet spills his milk. white puddles
well-up in the corners of his tray.
he is tender. he is upset.
          yet, I have nothing more
to comfort with.

Sudden Fiction

Summer rain rattles the downspouts.
I listen to Puccini, perfect music
for Sunday morning. From the window
I watch grass swell, so eager
to turn green.
                    My daughter, fresh
from napping, joins me. Rain fails
to interest her. Young butterfly—
her own ballet, to and fro,
with untrained pirouette—
just big enough to whirl
across rose-colored carpet.

I warn her not to dance too close
to the brick hearth. She collapses,
contemplating soot, and holds each palm
toward white oak cinders, then touches
a brass poker, rattles it against
a matching broom. *But, there's no fire.*
I pull her close and explain flame
is not today's danger:
                    that hearth is rough and hard.
Above the mantel, between fresh candles,
a landscape hangs—full of thin men
in red coats and black hats, riding

white stallions. Hounds cluster around
their polished boots. With bugle sounds,
a foxhunt begins.
                    She assures me
she will be careful if only
I will let her dance. Twisting from me,
her blonde hair twirls, frail arms weaving.
I reach around and close the firescreen's mesh.
Cold andirons wait, ornamented
by black owls with glass eyes, eager
for a chilled morning
in a February yet to come.

The Best Equipment

6:00 a.m. high tide:
tinged sun separates from sea and
gull calls peel back breakers
revealing bluefish and drum.
My son and I grip rods
that belonged to my grandfather.

My third bluefish beached,
he announces mine is the *lucky rod.*
My next fish on the taut filament,
I pass him the rod
and he reels in a baby drum.
I photograph him as he holds it high,

twirling on the line, black stripes
reflecting the sun. I assure him
both rods are his. Holding the big pole,
he swings it about the beach,
a shadow boxer measuring the distance.
to misty rainbows spilling onto the shore.

Middle C

I wrap my hand around hers
as we leave the specialist's office,
The fates have it: with all my child's beauties,
I am informed one ear needs surgery:
install a simple crease
so it will not protrude,
or define her, that is—
so she might resemble the rest,
reaffirm the diagnosis that determines *typical*.

At night, without poise of a first lesson,
she tinkers on the piano: from middle C,
practices scales using only white keys,
articulates a melody in minor chords.
Surprising herself, she redefines
the moment, locates unique
harmony playing a sharp or flat,
includes a wrinkle revealed
under the weight of notions.

Wintry Mix

Without warning, you alter my day—
wanting more firewood before
it becomes soggier with morning snow.
I see no reason to disembark the sofa.

Horizontal before the fireplace,
I offer you a quilt that needs no tinder—
but your posture is stern and straight.
Rising, I moan like only I can, still unconvinced.

Children sled outside, asphalt's black spine
revealed with each pass, down the block where
we sometimes stroll comfortable evenings,
or other everyday occasions when we leave,

yet return. Warm in a wool scarf I gave you,
you emerge smiling, extending leather gloves
to fend off spiders and splinters, and seize
some oak, encouraging me to hurry inside.

Cold Shoulder

Lavender speckle collects
on branches, in crotches
of the bleak trees. All appraisals

dread the trial of sleds, boot-prints,
children's laughter disrupting
compacted hush within the drifting:

plumbing the trunks, crooking
these impulsive jonquils' early flourish.
As I describe the snowfall's fracture,

you manage to squint at the frosted pane,
inquire about the hour, but
leave me as witness, to predict

no thaw, no impending parable
or solstice to reclaim this slim sun
that has lost its way.

Moving the Needle

You demand
proof the world spins
and stars blaze
at noon. It might
prove easier to reweave
clouds than recover
your trust in
my pledges.

I can only offer
this morning's promise
to unshackle what
entices you,
counsel against betrayals,
and, bolstered
by a faith,
let you go in peace.

Sunny Side Up!

My daughter rattles about the kitchen
scrambling morning calm. It is early for her,
when dreams should be reviewed, but

this morning she stands determined
to fry an egg: a new venture, a new risk
yet asks my advice on how it is done.

Crack the shell. *Pick out the shell.*
Pour into glass. *You're spilling it!*
Slice of butter in the pan. *Not melted yet!*
Pour egg in the pan. *You're spilling it!*
Wedge up the brown fringe. *Not yet!*

Flip it over once. *Not Yet!*
Slide it onto the plate. *Enjoy!*
I point out it is overcooked a bit.

She nods, pangs satisfied, and
asks for grape jelly since
we are in harmony over toast.

Legacy

Once upon a pastime,
I sketched faces in clouds,

and those discoveries remain
blurred in weary places:

some shrunken, some grayer.
Rousing my children to

the scent of rain, I explain
delicacy in a petal and the

bracing of a hummingbird's wing.
For them, each day seems complete.

Yet as evening looms over treeline,
and oak boughs swell in night-winds,

my hopeful muse emerges
on a faraway sea, and

describes their sailboat
where they will find peace

in a mermaid's lullaby,
their dreams christened

as they map a harbor where they may
one day moor their hearts.

Valentine's Day

In my realm
of priesthood, I raise my hand
against current plagues, stand eager
to heal the unworthy, appoint the insincere,
and hear confessions as I go.
Today's business: Baptism of the kingdom's princess.
And by my edict, all favorite sons
shall depart on a hike or to their heaven.

Only my prayers will cross her brow. To protect her is my charge alone.

I decree all
fair lads shall become dutiful warriors:
their tad of gristle will gird enough daring,
with tender courage wielded on ash swords.
Battlegrounds in uncut wheat, or
between the tracks in muddy lanes,
but their crimes uncommitted,
I allow no casualties.

Her blue eyes. Pearl buttons. Bleached cotton gown absorbs the noon light.

No harm
shall kiss her cheek.
Only my withering roses
will distract her heart, and
from behind my chamber drapes
I will command each honorable suitor
to some holy campaign, intentions undeclared,
so only I remain—

to battle her dragons and bless her dreams.

Calling Forth

As the moon pushes aside
crimson clouds, I discover
my son's tricycle
abandoned at the top of the drive—
primary-colored streamers,
the horn I never fixed.
I sprint about the block, bare
feet slapping the dirty asphalt.
I choke on bewildering fear:
in a blink of my careless eye,
he vanished behind an ageless sunset.
Fifteen minutes I yelp to him.

Then within my terror, I find my child—
and hold him, consoling panic,
as another cruel suffering clears.
Him safe beneath his blanket,
I rely on a bath to swallow
and soothe my blackened feet.
Dust tinges the cool water.
I must soak off evidence
of ground-in guilt.
I crouch, grateful for any
fair chance to wash away harm.

Standards

You extend one smooth palm
into sunlight on the hardwood floor.
With a bold finger, you mark carpet.
Clapping, cooing confirms your pleasure.
I cannot know the outline
of your dreams,
                    but I will help you etch
your landscape. I relate my boundaries:
wilting roses on the table, soggy newspapers,
paint-by-number views. A gloomy region
where sturdy brushstrokes stray.
But in your soft eyes, a fearless territory
converges. No parched color.
Nothing of stone. Receptive to imprint,
and content with a tiny handful
of a warm world.

Crow Talk

for Drew

Morning fog lifts.
Each hemlock's tip glistens,
as relics of snow crystals brighten.
From the porch, you caw
to some spirit unseen to me.

Disinterested with my quiet,
you erupt
        and,
                to your joy,
the white mountain responds.

It serenades through a black bird,
and sails on its wing. No account
does justice to morning sun like your words.
No trust exists more soothing than love for you,
but, for now, your conversation excludes me—

yet each smile encumbers my language:
with your call
         and coo
             and harmony
of the day's simple songs.

Fatherhood

The trunk gray with winter's kiss,
I hear the toll of an evening bell.
Call it peel or discordant clang,
like love, once struck, such brass,

its unceasing conscious prayer,
can never become un-rung.
While my child grows tall,
outlives my anxious words,

whether stumbling away angry,
or stunted at my shoulder,
I cannot create a legacy for him
only offer my easy-earned wisdom.

Will my vision perish unheralded
as he offers his new illumination:
beseeching me to never fret,
conceiving his way into night?

Distances

I recognize you in round faces
of a grouping of mothers in a café,
busy comparing small photographs.
Knowing you, such magic would be
in your command. Do you hide behind
any of their small eyes and thin smiles,
sharing their space
for an in-the-body moment?
If so, touch my starched sleeve.
No kisses, please—
that was never our style.
I pledge to reach back.

We always managed polite distance,
but triumphed with a stiff hug when
your mother died: she would have
insisted. You were vigilant—
nurturing as I would allow.
Me, the hesitant one, somehow
always expecting accommodations
to my timing.
          Oh, well.
                    I remained
absent during your ailing days—
we both know even then I would
have been little comfort. Good intentions
have no medicinal value.

                    My fingers,
that never mastered the piano, scratch
at bright ice over your epitaph, leaving
frigid granite still between us.
I listen for your lullaby's thaw, making
the attempt with your trait of patience.
Even now, the elements are on your side.

Goodnight, Mr. Moon

No man of fables,
I cannot tell you who he is,
distinguish any line of his cold complexion.
The brassy harvest moon remains
a mystery to me. My son, I can help you
identify the Sea of Tranquility,
spot dark regions of Mare Nubium, but
I see no smile, or pummeled dimples other fathers see.

Are those craters eyes, the gouges ears? Near
and full, October's moon should be an easy make.
Is that meteor slash a grin?
Today's questions have caught up with you,

slumped beside me in your car seat,
unbothered by any more debates.
I take this time to practice my clumsy arsenal
of answers. I am at a loss on many things—
my realm finite: a moonless sky,
uncluttered with your solar system of why or why-not.
After tucking in your small body, tugging
a blanket over your imagination, I stand by

Grandpa's drained lake. It curves between
glimmering beaches and gray stumps
where muskrats skitter. The shore stretches
far, lined with frames of leafless trees.

I teeter on the dock that crowns white sand
and map tomorrow, rehearse explanations
that must ring true as the clearest psalm.
We will hike the bogs and forsaken springs,
excavate leafy silt, poke driftwood
between cracks in the earthen dam. One-by-one
I will embrace your blaze of questions and
do my best to etch a face in tomorrow's sky.

The Gleaning

You accept comforting,
yield to each occurrence
while knowing so little
of the world. My body
crooks around you,
an unsure fortress at best.
I relate tales of pirates,
and treasure maps
to be stumbled upon.

This morning,
wide shrimp boats troll.
On the shore's edge,
pipers patrol the shallow pools
abandoned by high tide.
Shiny fish dart
landlocked dimensions.
Sand crabs burrow under
the thin wraps of waves.

Bravery and fear crest
each white cap that collapses
and spreads. Hemispheres of sea foam
dissolve into continents and
then to crust. Although
man christened this island,
he can claim no territory—
no lines alter
what the sea gives up.

You and I
curl together on the mattress
and I detail dawn,
and shale clouds,
and simple ripples in the sand:
you know so little of my soul.
All awaits your first step,
just there, beyond the sawgrass
and over the white dunes.

Certified Dancer

I know which things come easy to me—
if I log hours with a proper partner,
and practice awkward dance steps,

the day will come I am capable.
Courage and I practice in my room,
spin before mirrors to grade myself:

only going through motions, clumsy session
at best. Someday, for all to see, we must
waltz to my father's grave and, row after row,

rely on landmarks laid out like
footsteps on smooth green tile between
sleek stones and burnished emblems.

Today would have been his birthday.
I know my dancing has improved, and
am anxious to audition for him, but

this day, in my room, we step up, step back,
brush up on that all-important pivot.
We know which things come easy to me.

Streetlights

My child and her friends,
crunched into the backseat, wait:
the orange school bus, in pre-dawn
hush, except for girly giggles,
and occasional crow caw. Pattern

of north-stars that define our road
go dark, nova, one after the next:
bright pilots that guided me to this place,
an erected constellation, blacked-out,
conceding, like some snuffed season of love.

Fallen Boundaries

Searching out familiar stars,
I heard the collapse of a tree
sacrificed to midnight wind.
With sunrise, damage
becomes clear.
                    A white birch bough
sliced open an electric fence,
calming its spark.
Twists of barbed wire
curl between cedar posts.
Currents of unsheared lambs
trample the gap, risk the meadow lane
willing to be struck down.
Light warms the empty pasture

and buzzards circle the ditch.
I have learned not
to protect treasure in clay jars.
My children rumble,
about the yard shielding eyes with
plum-colored birthday balloons.
                    Silver maple's silhouette
rips our galvanized chain-link fence,
its gleam dripping into withered leaves.
Shadows crawl from vacant places.
Irises conduct eulogies in the garden.
A bared branch reveals
an abandoned wasp nest
hanging like a tattered skull.

Five O'clock Shadow

Homeward bound,
my day converges
at a traffic signal
where you take nothing on faith,
only cluster with
others seeking
permission to proceed,
dismiss the ravaging grind.

Waiting,
halted on this road taken,
I notice a slash of rainbow
burn through clouds—
a momentary slice flashing
between the slow burn
of pink and crimson.
I scan for other fragments
of green and magenta
refracted about the distance,

hoping to piece together
other colorful segments into
an entire arch,
locate any gold.
I move, but the horizon blurs,
now cluttered with empty boughs,
smudges of blue,
and motionless spires.

Coffee Talk

Sequestered in the basement,
abandoned to collect dust, I awarded
a cedar trunk den-space—
a cozy spot to share our communal coffee.
I stripped mint-green enamel and shellac,
burnished tight grain, polished brass.
Enhanced the lid with teak coasters and
colorful periodicals.

          Yet as our evenings pass,
children collide with the obstacle, dislodge
coasters; toys take over; magazines ripped, unread.
A television remote lies within reach.
We stuff the trunk with postponed thoughts,
bad poems and other ideas moths shy from.
No blankets or quilts: they have value
where there is chill.

          For now, we console
one another, anxious for that hour, television silent,
coasters can be located. When children tumble
outside past dusk; toys return to other rooms.
We will brew those pungent blends, steamy, sweet.
Enticed by soothing aromas, we will open the trunk,
prop back the lid and curl together on the couch
allowing solutions and intangibles their just time.

Soft Spots in the Stream

My son wants stories
at bedtime of when I was his age—
how I loved blue jays and feared shadows.
Back then,
           my sense of adventure
required the black mud bottom
of Burnt Mill Creek: stones, bream schools,
turtle beds. As frogs plunged in reeds,

my dad motioned open-handed
as I pleaded to stay close:
                  Trust the day.
He marched, under the gauze of Spanish moss,
fearless of water snakes. Water over my knees,
he taught me creek walking, how to balance
up slick banks with willow spindles and cypress knees.
I emerged, baptized with solutions.

                      Once home,
he lacked answers,
those waning days when things unraveled,
when he often clenched his fist.
He bogged down with questions,
brooding in his recliner:
                Keep with it,
the best he could offer.

Now, I escort my son
off to sleep, with his unresolved
problems and prayers, and at times I shrug,
unable to help him add things up.
But in his murky waters,
I part the surface, and
search with him for
soft spots in the stream.

The Shade That Saves Me

I grace the shadow
of the happy people
and the weeping cherry.

Among laughing children,
balls, bats, and lemonade
provide order to the day.

My fingers sift torn soil
even earthworms have abandoned.
My imprint lingers

with the fallow clods
that long for planting,
that long for those colors

and songs that gorge
the tulips, hydrangea, and rose.
Between crepe myrtle stalks

plied faces stare back
as I withdraw into the shade
that saves me.

Robins shield nests within
the privet hedge when
my careless phrases emerge

as the offspring of the beast
lurks to reveal the edges
of my weakness.

Gestation Period

We will move soon, adapt to new
quarters, new neighbors, new trees.
The years I borrowed breath from this house
I portrayed fool as friend, mate as lover,
son as father, but each performance was bound
by common twining

              It is November:
I expect to stare through mottled panes
onto a frosted lawn. Carved pumpkins
on the porch gleam like charmed goblins.
Sycamore leaves scurry between curbs
of the iced street.

                 Songbirds departed,
their nests, revealed, knot maple forks—
I scour holly shrubs for today's paper, wind
on my face like her kiss that hardened overnight.
My children dream in this house
in a room designed as a parlor—a room

where the first owner's daughter was courted,
or perhaps his mother's wake was held.
I promise them so much while they sleep
still and violet in moonlight. Cribbed,
they are captured in bright dreams.
Soon this house will bear
the rage of new confessions.

In our fresh surrounding,
                 in untested chambers,
my children will spring up,
                 delightful and erect.
Our new yard's trees will lose remaining leaves,
dislodged by the new buds' demanding.

III

That Rain We Needed

Spice Garden

for Jan

The brown snake has emerged from winter-sleep,

rested and supple, ready to shed. You

crouch, deliberate above the smooth stones

edging your spice garden. Late-morning frost

slinks back to bristles, under cool shadows.

Your stiff brittle patch persists without bloom,

with no hesitation, you swing the scythe,

bitter judgment served on the faltering.

Clear verdict slashed around mud-covered boots,

before high-noon heat, you stockpile the stalks.

Love Letter to My Wife

Destined to never have ample answers,
or honor every promise made in passion
or pretending, we go about family business,
and for the most part meet schedules.
How do we accomplish vital stuff with a glance?
Without belly laughs? No whispering?

We allow no time for such playfulness,
just rely on divine intrusion—you made
time to bear children, and teach them songs.
You quiz me when we need answers.
As you told me you would be traveling,
I hold your photograph. Fingers wipe off dust:

You fit well in that polished boundary
where my life can be framed.
We have chosen art for the walls.
It hangs in these caverns like bright angels
attending some colorless plane of our life together.
In our best of times, we tumble in yellow grass

like Matisse's lovers in *Joy of Life*.
And if the shape of love is not a masterpiece,
then I am left alone with a collection of empty mattes
to restock with happiness: that familiar filler quickly overlooked.
So tonight, you are away, with those same singing children.
Without you, I spin baskets full of questions.

I create supper from the icebox and jot you a note
all about it. Coffee maker set for breakfast,
I pledge to fetch you coffee every sunrise,
and soften it with Irish cream. Practice
over and over until that numb morning
I forget.

Recurring Dream

I stumble from a ladder,
mis-stepping through a rung—
preoccupied, peering up
to some lofty destination,
a change of venue for star-gaz_ng.

During the thrill of ascension,
I loosen my grip, testing
if some trinity might rescue me.
And I fall, dream after dream,
each time I reach the REM—

stratum by stratum, through ice crystals.
Snagged in the belly of combed clouds
I release all I am into wind
free-falling as a piano tinkles
a light-hearted etude.

Summer Vacation

After showering, you emerge
from steam, matted in the doorway,
perfect Venus,
arms intact, motioning
between folds of blue cotton.
I peel the towel
from your bright body
and squeeze your essence from it.

You purr with thoughts
of last night's white wine
beaded across your body,
hum an exotic tune
that recalls how spring passed
us without incident, left behind
nothing we have not learned
to take in stride.

        In early morning,
my mind ponders new approaches
to the upcoming season, considers
if my imagination—once solid as marble—
has seen its finer days.
        My eyes ache,
sore from Thursday's eclipse.
Of course, I glanced, eyes unshielded:
another reality
better off ignored. Merciful
to know which blindness to expect.

Burdens of Proof

For some reason
I obligated myself to forge
grand comfort for us—
so ambitious, so smart—
spun mythical formulas
and bland mechanics
to restructure The Science of Love.
Weight of my notions

spread upon us, romance slumbers,
a diffused pastime. Flat. Efficient.
You sleep, silent love, within reach,
draped with a smooth sheet
like a burnished Greek bust,
the plum of a Romanticist's study,
ready to celebrate, ready
for a scarlet morning.

Covenant

I dwell in a graceless garden,
eager to align with spring.
And as with any abandoned component,
I long for my true mother.
Through winter,
                    I have sifted
sterile covenants piled in place
for my protection. Another nameless
season passes—while grateful
for considerations—I stand ready now,
willing to engage her sin and sorrow.
Some things must be accepted,
embraced for what they are.
Those fear-frozen folks provide
no new answers for me,
                    or her.
In these early hours, from behind glass,
I believe she watches red lights blink
on the cloud bellies, and senses
I am close. Tomorrow has come—
with it firm forgiveness. Acquainted
with life's tests for tragedy,
buried in frost,
                    I hide from sun:
lost in this face of her nameless child.
Our solution twists through
the garden trellis, blooming
in the explosion of a rose.

Communion

This silence, discernible,
attempts to renovate all wreckage
before daybreak. The morning rain's
shards echo, etch my renewed wish,
carves fresh hearts from a harvest moon,
calms my daughter's midnight mood.

One day, we will wake to need each other—

deep in those withered months before winter,
interrupt her reverie in green fields, or frolic
in meadows of poppies, and unite again
on a low summit of hissing snow. Only then
will she appreciate our journeys back
and let me hug her for the proper farewell.

The Color of Things

A trace of your image escapes
from darkness. Between
sundown and REM, you visit me:

nightgown drooped on the bedpost,
that marvelous thud of lace
on the hardwood floor, toes burrowing

beside me beneath the blanket's down.
You, so often sequestered in the study
with cigarettes and Russian Tea,

travel the immaculate distance
mapped in memory, plotted only with love's
intuition. I inventory lines in your face,

validations of the pattern that makes you up.
You remind me, *It's not the shape of things,
but their color.*

Peripheral Vision

for Patches

From my corner of the room,
inside the corner of the sash,
I witness autumn's bronze
in windblown frenzy.
It recalls shared Saturdays when
you tussled in the yard with the children.
They shouted my name to join in
and toss your ball so you galloped
in that clumsy gait beside them,
stirring up leaves I had just raked.

I still inhale freshness of their hair,
listen for stumbling, and wait
for that skinned-knee wail,
and to heed your feeble bark,
that unease in your brown eyes.
Sunlit sibling squabbles echo,
while your silhouette guards
the French doors to the porch,
sniffing the shears, energized,
hearing giggles in the dormant garden.

Grown away into independence
since we raised them to be strong,
like leaves on breeze, they scramble
from us, tumbling forward, right or less right.
I search for you
bedside each morning, at the noon hour
as we shared lunch, you content
with my crumbs, and always
available for a pat on the head,
stroke of the tail, and to chase the wind.

Keeping a Journal

This house, still and creaking
from the cold, hosts much more
than wishes. At my desk, I prepare
all manner of morning. Sifting notes
clipped to more notes,
                              I uncover a photograph
of a Mexican father, flanked by a wife
and a gravedigger. In mist, they process
up a hill on a cobblestone lane
fronted by stucco cottages and shops.
Porches lean and cover sleeping hounds.
His son's small coffin strapped across his shoulders,
the father wears his Sunday hat,
struggling with the new balance.
He repeats answers he cannot pass on
to his boy.
                 I study veins in my palm.
Switching places with this father,
one hand would hold my daughter,
the other his broken mother.
Could I muster grace to stake
Easter flowers on his grave?
                              For now,
I race my son to maturity: to the first
fine hair on his chin, to that handsome grin
the day I notice he is worldly, being there
each day to help him solve his moments.

I vow to jot only the positive word,
sidestep tragic matters, take the high road.
For today, I press the book cover tight
—that photo sealed between random pages—
and creep through the shadowed house,
avoiding hollows poised to corrupt,
accepting which victories
I must live without.

Red Planet

We speed to the shore's horizon
and I am certain
there must be more to us
as we leave the aura of tiny wars.
Our calling lies closer to the sun,
on a world where love and longing fuse,

not into white-hot anguish but
into a peaceful absolute.
When I love you, black sky's discord
brightens washed with stars, disorder calmed.
Sun, close enough to evaporate doubt,
warms our beach where we fight no theory,

do not cling to constrewed arguments.
Content, we absorb sparkles in sandwash,
white foam abandoned on the beach
by ancient crests. Here we will wait,
shoulder to shoulder, wrapped
in laughter, poised for radiance.

Seven Colors

Sunset Beach 2013

My love has her knacks:
locates four leaf clovers in any field,
collects sharks teeth from any shore.

In a latticed chair, I recline at water's edge,
let foam brine surge around my ankles.
Then I select another crest off-shore,
white cap absorbed into swell,
into the heave, intangible until it breaks.

I cock back my head to enjoy sea spray.
Enjoying that faint kiss, I see a rainbow
encircling noon sun—no beginning,
no end I distinguish expected colors,
without origin, no chance at a pot of gold.

Waving to my love, pointing up,
she is awed too, but returns to her book,
pages to caress, content, her blanket
on glaring sand. I beckon her to the water
to share this rainbow before a next cloud.

I offer sand dollars and conchs, but
she has her chapters, her metaphors—
content without my colors to shade her day.

Her Blue Plate

Strangers sift our devalued treasures
scattered about the driveway—
all on sale. Bargains. Bargains.
Once-prized, now clutter,
boxed like idle arguments
in the damp basement
among camel crickets and barren webs.

We let it go, time has paid its price,
still I feel an occasional tug—
a child's toy from Santa
that brightened their eye,
or a designer garment
now out-of-style. All escape
down the drive to better circumstances.

My mother had a smooth blue plate.
Youthful, I betrayed it
to a dealer who knew value.
Embossed with a white bird
perched on bamboo,
she displayed it
on my grandfather's desk.

Detached onto a stranger's mantel
or buffet, abandoned in the rain,
secluded in a cedar closet,
which of today's items,
with their unknown glamour,
will I crave again?
Who will relay their histories?

Already, I miss each toy, and
I picture her blue plate sheen—
its fired ceramic cool
to the touch, the exotic bird
warbling a serenade
the new owners will never hear.

And She Cries Every Sunday

We rise and rehash the night before—
too much drinking, too little dancing.
This pattern ingrained,
we trash the rest. She must
be mighty. She must console herself.

On a pew, side by side, we sing
from separate hymnals, wrapped in
silence no gospel can bring forth.
We sit and stare before the pulpit, pondering
compassion. Baffled by cause and effect,

surrounded by faces of Eden, we
share no epistle or benediction,
sacrament or noon bell.
And she cries every Sunday,
after all the hymns and hallelujahs,
our epiphany to unfold in stanzas yet to chant.

Litmus

My wife's Hydrangea blooms
again this year. Overwhelming
the natural-area niche I created

border of salt-treated cross ties,
double-ground pine mulch,
fertilized to thrive in minimal sun.

Her behemoth grew from a clipping
from another's garden overpowered
by their heft. Communal effort,

of sorts, but compromising my sense
of how a summer backyard blossoms.
Voltaire gave advice to tend it—

my way unaltered, and unobtrusive.
When I want blue, I plant blue.
Yellow shall be yellow, and red red.

I declare for caladiums, and lambs ear,
and snap dragons. Maybe a daisy or two.
pull the weeds, prune the puny.

Yet when nourished by another, she has
her way with me, redefines my borders,
redesigns my notion of blending,

introduces grays, and prompts our love
for gardening to become a patch
of that untested province we hold close.

The Void of Conformity

Pinot Noir swells my wine glass
as water does the womb. Each droplet
perfects a purpose, each nuanced
toward fulfillment of the terms.

I snap apart the hourglass,
pouring its sand into my palm
as if I could contain the silicate,
rearrange it into an aggregate instant.

Yet when we abandon safer dimensions,
bright reveries mangled and reshaped,
they ease into a role that they must serve:
dreams displaced, and revised each night.

Sunlight engorges our cluttered bedroom.
The blinds slice shadows, breaching
the realm where we embrace,
across our love that re-forms time after time.

Refraction

I crank cantilevered kitchen windows apart,
allow in scents that make the bees buzz,
yellow finches flutter in pairs. Garish light sends
spiders to shadows and moths tighten into eaves.

The motionless room is dull without your prism
above the sill, rotating slowly on plumb twine,
refracting light that pierces past un-rustled branches,
exploding sunrise with hues to enliven us.

I ache for its laser-drawn tints onto cool walls,
perfect lines across these things we have collected,
over the silent treasures we highlight within
false frames and gilded borders like hushed bark.

You took the crystalline shape down to wash the pane.
Smudges and smears emerged from seasons
when the sunrise ushered no cleansing
but endurance through another harsh instant.

I find the polished beacon knotted on the counter,
set aside with the dishcloths and stray cookbooks.
Its charm huddled, awaiting your grace to re-hang it, and
careen colors about us, reviving our departed blush.

Drip Line

Shade of the wild cherry tree,
where fruit softens and sours,
fit for grubs and summer swarms:
my children join me, eager
to pluck a sand pail of ripe cherries,
those still with a pop of surprise.
Their harvest clings to limbs,
drooping with extra weight
of a cooling-down shower.

I urge my helpers—*take your time,*
don't choose by color but by feel.
They listen, yet peep to the tree's crown,
to the tender yield, mapping out
which offshoots will get them there.
I let them go
                    and they scurry
within the shadow, locating laden stems.
Bending branches onto their heads,
rain clinging to leaves speckles their shoulders.
Ripe faith resting with green limbs,
they ascend, reckless—
scrambling to the bounty.
Where sunset penetrates bough,
an occasional bright face flares.
I move about messy fruit
in the grass beneath them,
and cull what worms
would shred by night.

Lost Frequency

I heard Hendrix rampage, and
the bliss of blues buzz by Cream.
George Harrison's twang.
Their strapped-on-Fender solid bodies
or a hollow white Gibson that
liberated John Lennon's anthems.
Through it all, I clamped headphones
tight to never miss a distorted note,
sealing out that parental contorted rote:
TURN IT DOWN!
From a backseat I heard the backbeat
and cranked Pete Towshend on a Stratocaster
or the Funkadelics on a Ghetto Blaster.
That 60's music, the hard kind, like first love,

rocks me awake now each grown-up sun-up
as your roll did once each night. As if
holding the un-flexing whammy bar,
your dexterous fingers wah-wahed
my midnights into resolute slumber.
But these days, my listening has been lessened,
intimate frequencies fallen mute.
Our modulations fewer and further between,
I hum each chorus with fading fervor
while your notes reverb in my refrain.
As ear-buds drown out ambient throb,
I am left with only fretful melody, each tone
beckoning my trembling timbre, yet knowing
one day the ranges within reach shall fall tone-deaf too.

Backscatter

I finally visit my grandfather's farm.
Sturdy wind sways the pecan grove,
in unison, boughs iced-over.

Holly shrubs slump, shiny and green.
Distant acres idle while thickets
encroach on the vineyard's edge.

I never helped him pluck grapes,
but now enjoy most wines. Parched,
in hiatus, I salute late-day shadows,

debate my off-season seclusion,
bleak with snowy whispers
I deflect into the bramble,

where thorns glisten awaiting
the scythe. Sun twitches, but only
radiance from his good earth

can thaw these bristly acres,
answer their lingering regret,
eulogies resolved by the night.

Thyme

Your sandals by the door,

the kitchen blushes with fragrance.
Poised at the blue counter,
hair cinched back with white ribbon,
you invite sunrise through the window.

Feet cross at the ankle.
Among ceramic canisters
stocked with aphrodisiacs
for my appetite, leaf by leaf,

you crumble dried spice
from the sparse garden
of thyme, oregano, and sage.
Rolling them off their stems,

your fingers become tart.
I have my pastimes, but—never
the gardener—marvel at your yield
ground into small pimento jars

you saved. You pile bare stems
on a paper towel. I rest my chin
on a shoulder and affection's seed
rolls down your soft furrow to chest,

burrows, content to flourish here.

Solar Eclipse

Noontime shadows constrict to picket fences.
Snowbirds consider distant oak branch call.
Clocks chime midmorning dissonance.

The cock cannot crow in this ill-timed dark.
Blinded hawk, beak and talons prone,
discerns his choices on the breeze.

This is not an Easter morning, yet
the flaxen moon guarding my tomb of guilt
has rolled back, and hovers above the swale.

Strike your candle: illuminate my dim crossing.
Offer wine that douses more than thirst.
Be flint to fuse the gilded light in our cupped palms.

Favorite Things

Brandy Alexander before midnight.
Cigarettes on our screened porch watching rain.
Perhaps I will postpone my haircut
just because you like me shaggy

Your blind spots and beloved things:
where your random darlings abide,
disappointments are pardoned because
our children do no wrong.

A divining curtain hangs between us,
too heavy to be moved by wind,
yet delicate enough to sway with a whisper.
Evasion can be the better part of valor.

Secret Burial

for Sushi

In a windless hour,
she demands last rites:
without wailing, stares
through crisp leaves,
incisors poised for a midnight cat-fight.
Beneath the porch, adjacent
to a scattering of cardinal wings
and squirrel skulls, I search her for a mangle,
a puncture, any evidence
to ease my weary hereafter.

Like a Halloween cut-out,
the gray cat slides onto the shovel.
Unceremonious, alone at the burial site:
my wife, the neighbors, all
must know of this on my terms,
at my pace. I will control death's toll.

Disturbing the loose loam,
I am finished with my old house cat
that was forced to learn to roam.
I shall not trust in freedom again—
there are things that should remain bound.
In urban distance,
                    her litter mate,
who fares well outside, witnesses
my secrecy, burying love
with such efficiency.
She was a crystal of his flesh.
He grooms his furry chest,
king on his savannah,
refusing to risk the asphalt street
and return home to pardon me.

Just Reading

My love's
new Ming lamp is odd:
crowned with a green shade,
embossed with red and blue birds.

She positioned it atop
her chestnut dresser,
beside the silent phone.

To rummage room for it,
she jostled texts, sifted junk mail,
hid away Dear Diary.

So nights when sleep is scarce
that royal lamp waits handy:
jar-shaped source

of late-night bliss.
I always hoped my loyal
passion might prove plenty
to make our bedroom bright.

Tomato

I pass my time well,
but if a man is worth his salt,
he will learn his season.

I hope to die some indigo night—
un-diagnosed—preferably,
in my tomato garden.

I wait content in this fertile space.

I water each vine.
Spray rattles the dry leaves
and collects on stem bristles.

Tonight I know, plucking
ripe fruit is kind: by autumn,
so much rots, ignored.

Fealty

In your land of trellises and gardens,
simple things satisfy. Lucky for me—
a man too impatient for hybrids—
my roses cling to the fence, threaded
wiry and wild, volunteers . . .
the Knockout breed: random color,
thorns to barb, beget the blood.

When we dance, I master the misstep,
prove clumsy, impatient on our path.
Even, as you lead, I will win no ribbon,
no medallion to polish. Twinking on toes,
or on my back, I pledge to practice
whenever you beckon, each step, again,
and again, until my motions make you beam.

I count movements, yearning to earn your blush,
peel back petals of your bloom, explore
your marbled spirit, eager to be plucked.
I will follow. I will lead. I will, I will,
as it pleases you, my gardener, my partner,
nurture your blossoms, unbind your red ribbons,
and yield to your dominion in the spaces I adore.

That Rain We Needed

Dogwood petals splattered across the driveway
gleam, knocked off by overnight torrents.
Easter flowers breathe, now embedded

along hedgerow. Your herb garden sprouts
preferred garnishes. Dark granite stones
surround this haven, white veins dividing millennia.

Dandelions, those not yanked or scolded,
have receded until another season. We wait
with chilled teas and books we preferred to finish.

Fescue beams lush. The daffodils droop
from mid-morn showers. I sip my coffee
and Kahlua behind porch screens and rock,

at ease in my decision that today we should relax . . .
let jazz simmer, allowing Saturday's meld into
Sunday . . . audition new favorites for our soundtrack

of this nurtured life, its polite ideals
and unexpected blooms, all properly cropped
and savored in scattered vases.

SAM BARBEE grew up in Wilmington, North Carolina, and studied creative writing at University of North Carolina – Wilmington. His poems have appeared in *Crucible, Asheville Poetry Review, The Southern Poetry Anthology VII: North Carolina, Potato Eyes, Georgia Journal, St. Andrews Review, Main Street Rag, Iodine,* and *Pembroke Magazine,* among others. His first collection of poems, *Changes of Venue,* was published by Mount Olive Press in 1997. He has been a featured poet on North Carolina Public Radio Station WFDD, and he received the 59th Poet Laureate Award from the North Carolina Poetry Society for his poem "The Blood Watch." He lives in Winston-Salem, North Carolina, with his wife Jan.

www.ingramcontent.com/pod-product-compliance
Lightning Source LLC
LaVergne TN
LVHW041341080426
835512LV00006B/565